Welcome to Russia

Meredith Costain   Paul Collins

Chelsea House Publishers
1974 Sproul Road, Suite 400
Broomall, PA 19008–0914

The Chelsea House world wide web address is www.chelseahouse.com

Library of Congress Cataloging-in-Publication Data Applied for.
ISBN 0-7910-6549-9

First published in 2000 by
Macmillan Education Australia Pty Ltd
627 Chapel Street, South Yarra, Australia, 3141

Copyright © Meredith Costain and Paul Collins 2000

Edited by Miriana Dasovic
Text design by Goanna Graphics (Vic) Pty Ltd
Page layout by Goanna Graphics (Vic) Pty Ltd
Cover design by Goanna Graphics (Vic) Pty Ltd
Printed in Hong Kong

Acknowledgements
The author and the publisher are grateful to the following for permission to reproduce copyright material:

Cover photograph: Matrioshka dolls, © Blaine Harrington.

Auscape, p. 20 © Ferrero-Labat, p. 21 (top) © S Cordier, p. 21 (bottom) © Ferrero-Labat;
Angela Costain, pp. 10 (bottom), 30; Great Southern Stock, p. 7 (top) © N Offler, pp. 13 & 18
© Jim Hooper, p. 19 (bottom) © N Offler, p. 22 (left) © Pho N E, p. 24 © N Offler, p. 26
© Jim Hooper, p. 29; Blaine Harrington, pp. 5, 6 (top & bottom), 10 (top), 11 (top & bottom),
12 (left), 15 (top), 22 (right), 23, 27 (top & bottom); Angela Jones, pp. 7 (bottom), 8, 25, 30;
Lonely Planet Images, p. 12 (right) © John Noble, p. 14 © Lee Foster, pp. 15 (bottom), 19 (top) & 28
© John Noble; Sport. The Library, p. 9 © Dmitri Radchenko; PhotoDisc, p. 30.

While every care has been taken to trace and acknowledge copyright the publishers tender their apologies for any accidental infringement where copyright has proved untraceable.

Contents

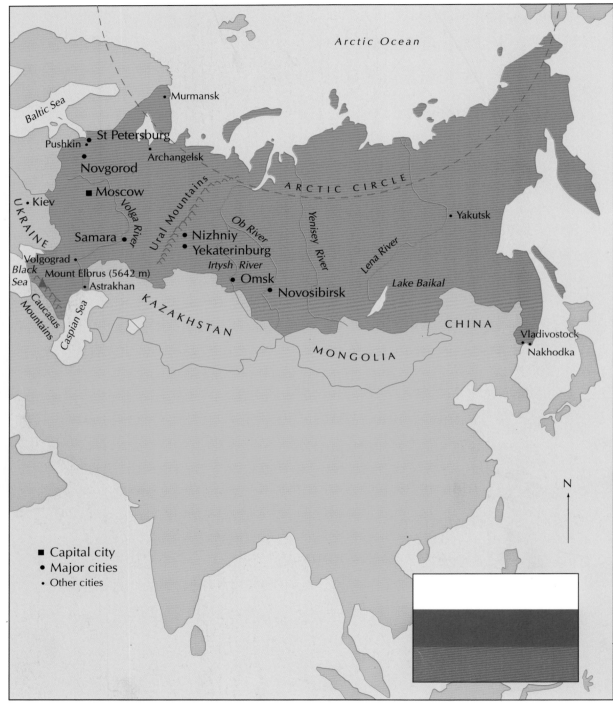

Arctic Ocean

Baltic Sea

• Murmansk

St Petersburg

Pushkin •

• Archangelsk

Novgorod

UKRAINE • Kiev

■ Moscow

ARCTIC CIRCLE

• Yakutsk

Volga River

Ural Mountains

Ob River

Yenisey River

Lena River

Samara •

• Nizhniy
• Yekaterinburg

Volgograd •

Irtysh River

Black
Sea

Mount Elbrus (5642 m)

• Astrakhan

• Omsk

Lake Baikal

Caucasus
Mountains

Caspian Sea

KAZAKHSTAN

• Novosibirsk

CHINA

MONGOLIA

Vladivostock •

Nakhodka

N

■ Capital city
• Major cities
• Other cities

Welcome to Russia!

Zdravstvuyte! My name is Tatiana and I come from St. Petersburg, in Russia.

My country, Russia, is the biggest in the world. It covers over 17 million square kilometers (6.6 million square miles), about one-ninth of the world's land area. Russia extends from the Arctic Ocean in the north to the Black Sea in the south, and from the Pacific Ocean in the east to the Baltic Sea in the west. It is divided by the Ural Mountains into a European region in the west, and an Asian region in the east.

For many years, Russia was part of a huge country called the Soviet Union. The government tried to tell people what to do, and how to live their lives. In 1991, the Soviet Union broke up. Then Russia, along with 10 other former republics, formed a group called the Commonwealth of Independent States, or CIS. People are now more free to live their lives the way they want, and to follow their old traditions and customs.

Our flag changed in 1991. It used to have a gold star and a hammer and sickle on a red background. Now it has three horizontal stripes of white, blue and red.

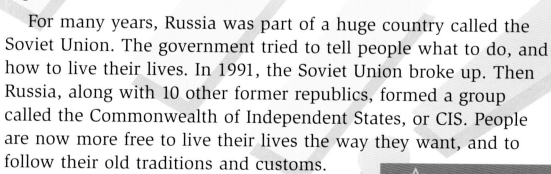

Family life

St. Petersburg is in the northwest of Russia. It is Russia's second largest city, and used to be called Leningrad. St. Petersburg was once the capital of the **Russian Empire**. Many beautiful palaces, churches and squares were built by Czar Peter 1, who was known as Peter the Great.

My family lives in a small, rented apartment in a high-rise building. There are many apartment buildings like this in St. Petersburg. Some of them are very crowded, with two families living together. Our apartment has two bedrooms, a living room, a small kitchen, a bathroom and a balcony. I love to sit outside on the balcony and draw the people I see on the city streets below me.

Our apartment has a small balcony. Sometimes it is hard living so close to so many other people.

Family friends get together for a meal.

I have an older brother, Alexei. He is at university studying to be a doctor. My mother, Svetlana, is a teacher, and my father, Mikhail, lectures at the university. My uncle Sergei lives with us too. He works as a journalist on the city newspaper.

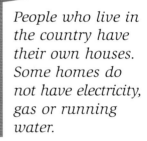

After school I watch TV, play chess with Alexei, draw pictures, or play with my friend Dasha. She lives in the apartment next door. Dasha has a tabby cat called Coco. I would like a cat too, but my mother says it would make too much mess, and she would end up having to take care of it every day. Maybe she will change her mind soon.

People who live in the country have their own houses. Some homes do not have electricity, gas or running water.

My grandmother meets with her friends every day.

School

Children in Russia start school at the age of seven. It is compulsory for children to attend school for 10 years, until they are 17. Many children spend a few years at kindergarten before they start school.

We go to school six days a week. The school day starts at 8:30 a.m. and ends at 2:30 p.m. At primary school we learn Russian, maths, geography, history, social studies, physical education and a foreign language. At my school we learn English. We stay at primary school until we are 11, then move up to secondary school.

There are three types of secondary schools. Most students go to a general school, where they study the basic subjects, plus science and computer studies. My brother Alexei went to a 'vocational school', where he concentrated on science subjects like chemistry and physics. I am working hard at my art so that I will be chosen for a special school for artists.

After secondary school, students either leave to find a job, or go to college or university to study to become doctors, engineers or lawyers.

Grade 2 students admire their finger puppets, a gift from a visiting Australian teacher.

Sports and leisure

Most Russians enjoy playing chess. Children are taught how to play the game as soon as they are old enough to understand the different rules. In summer, lots of people play open-air chess games in parks or on quiet street corners. A crowd gathers to watch the games. Many Grand Masters and world champions have come from Russia. Our most famous players include Garry Kasparov and Anatoly Karpov.

People also enjoy collecting stamps, going to the movies and visiting museums and art galleries, such as the Hermitage here in St. Petersburg.

It is cheap to travel in Russia. Many people go to Moscow or to seaside resorts at the Black Sea for their annual holidays. In northwestern Russia, where winters are cold and snowy, people go skiing, ice-skating, sleigh-riding and reindeer-racing. Others carve ice sculptures, or build towns and fortresses out of snow. Some people even cut holes in the ice and go swimming!

Most Russian people play some form of organized sport, such as volleyball, basketball or ice hockey. Soccer is the most popular, to play and watch!

Russian culture

People who live in Moscow think they are the most cultured people in Russia! There are many great theaters, concert halls, cinemas, libraries, art galleries and museums. On national holidays, many plays and concerts are free, so that everybody, rich or poor, is able to enjoy Russian culture.

Some people say that Russian ballet is the best in the world. In Moscow, operas and ballets are performed at the famous Bolshoi Theater. St. Petersburg is also famous for its ballet. The Imperial Ballet School produced the famous dancers Anna Pavlova and Vaslav Nijinsky, and the choreographers Marius Petipa and Mikhail Fokine.

The Moscow Circus is famous.

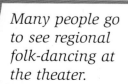

Many people go to see regional folk-dancing at the theater.

Hand-painted Matrioshka dolls. Each doll contains smaller dolls inside.

Famous Russian composers include Peter Tchaikovsky and Igor Stravinsky. Anton Chekhov is our most famous **playwright**. His plays have been translated into many different languages, and performed in theaters around the world. Other famous writers include Boris Pasternak and Leo Tolstoy. Alexander Solzhenitsyn, who wrote about life in labor camps in Siberia, won the Nobel Prize for Literature in 1970. He was **exiled** from Russia from 1974 to 1994.

Russia is also famous for its **icons**, which are religious pictures painted on wooden panels. Many of our churches are decorated with bright colors and 'onion-domes', which are often painted gold.

The Catherine Palace at Pushkin, south of St. Petersburg, has typical Russian 'onion-dome' spires on its roof.

Festivals and religion

When Russia was part of the **communist** country called the Soviet Union, people were afraid to openly follow a religion. But now many of the churches and monasteries that were closed have been opened again, and people are free to follow their beliefs. Most Russians belong to the Russian Orthodox Church, but there are many other religions. Most cities have a Jewish synagogue, and a mosque for Muslims.

Easter is the most important festival for the Russian Orthodox Church. Everyone goes to church on the midnight before Easter Sunday. The priest dresses up in fancy robes, and the church is lit by candles. At the end of the service, we take our candles outside, and walk around the churchyard singing Easter hymns.

Most Christians in Russia are members of the Russian Orthodox Church.

A wedding party outside one of Russia's many beautiful churches.

Carol singers at Christmas time.

Then we go home for a special Easter feast. We eat roast meat, a special Easter cake called *kulich*, and a rich, cheesy dessert called *pashka*. Sometimes we do not get to eat until two or three o'clock in the morning!

We have our Christmas on the 7th of January. It is a quiet family holiday. On Christmas Eve, we wait for the first star to appear in the sky. Then we light candles and lamps, and sit down to a special Christmas supper. My favorite dishes are *kutya*, which is wheat porridge served with honey, and stewed apples or pears. After supper we visit our godparents, who give us Christmas presents.

New Year is a great time for parties. At the Kremlin in Moscow, 50,000 children crowd into the square each year. Grandfather Frost and the Snow Maiden visit with gifts for everyone. People wear fancy dress, dance, and go ice-skating. Some people go for a ride on a *troika*, a sleigh drawn by three horses.

Russian festivals and holidays

New Year's Day	January 1
Christmas Day (Russian Orthodox Church)	January 7
Easter	March/April
May Day	May 1
Victory Day	May 9
National Day	June 12
Harvest festivals	July/August
Peace and Harmony Day	November 7

Food and shopping

When Russia was a communist country, it was hard to buy food. Shops had a 'three-line' system. First you had to wait in one line to order the item you wanted to buy. The shop assistant took the item from the shelf, wrote out a ticket and gave it to you. Then you had to wait in another line at the cash register, so the cashier could take your money and stamp your ticket. Finally you took your stamped ticket back to the shop assistant, who wrapped your item and gave it to you. It took a lot of time just to buy bread!

Some shops, such as toyshops, bookshops and some clothing and food shops, still use this system. But now we have Western-style department stores and supermarkets as well, so shopping is much easier! Even so, shops often run out of food and goods, and people still wait in long lines.

Many Russian people must wait in long lines to buy food.

GUM is Moscow's largest department store. It is on one edge of Red Square, opposite the Kremlin.

Meals

Breakfast is a quick, simple meal. We usually eat rye bread and cheese, and drink tea. We eat our main meal of the day at lunchtime. This is usually a dish made from meat and potatoes, and other vegetables. After this we might eat some fruit, a piece of cake, or pancakes with jam and sour cream called *bliny*. At suppertime, we have a lighter meal: maybe *borscht* (soup made from beetroot), cabbage and sausage, followed by little meat pasties called *piroshki*.

Russians love to drink sweet black tea. We always keep a metal urn called a samovar on the dining table. It contains boiling water for the tea. The teapot sits on the top of the samovar to keep warm.

A street stall sells local produce.

Make *pashka*

After we have been to church at Easter, we go home and eat a huge feast to celebrate the end of **Lent**. We eat roast meat and *pashka*, a rich Easter dessert.

Ask an adult to help you prepare this dish.

What you need:

- 500 grams (2 cups) butter
- 7 egg yolks
- 2 cups sugar
- 1 kilogram (4 cups) cottage cheese
- 250 milliliters (1 cup) cream, whipped
- 1 teaspoon vanilla flavoring
- 1 cup raisins
- 1/2 cup nuts
- 1/2 cup lemon rind, grated
- some candied fruit and fresh flowers for decoration

What to do:

1 Cream the butter with an electric mixer, or by hand.

2 In a separate bowl, beat the egg yolks until they are thick. Slowly add the sugar and beat well.

3 Spoon the egg and sugar mixture into the bowl with the creamed butter. Mix it well.

4 Drain any liquid from the cottage cheese, then push it through a sieve. Add the cheese to the butter and egg mixture. Blend well.

5 Fold in the whipped cream, vanilla, raisins, nuts and lemon rind.

6 Wrap the mixture in a wet cloth. Place a weight on top. Put the dessert in the fridge to chill for 48 hours.

7 Take off the cloth. Decorate the cake with candied fruit and fresh flowers. Serve cut into slices.

Make your own *pysanky*
(decorated Easter eggs)

We give our family and friends decorated eggs at Easter time. During the Easter feast, we have an egg-knocking competition. If our egg doesn't crack when we knock it against someone else's, it is the winner!

Ask an adult to help you with this.

What you need:

- eggs
- a pin
- a saucepan
- vinegar
- food coloring or food dye
- poster paint and fine brushes

What to do:

1. Pierce the flatter end of the eggs with a pin to release the air in the air sac. This will stop the eggs from cracking as they cook.
2. Boil the eggs for 10 minutes.
3. When the eggs have cooled, clean them by gently rubbing their surface with vinegar.
4. Carefully place the eggs in food coloring or dye until the shells are coloured.
5. Allow the dye to dry.
6. Paint brightly colored dots, stripes or wavy lines on your eggs.

Landscape and climate

Russia is a huge country, covering 11 time zones. When it is breakfast time in Vladivostock, in the far east, it is already time for me to go to bed here in St. Petersburg!

Except for the Caucasus Mountains in the south, and the low-rising Ural Mountains, most of Russia is flat. The land in the far north, bordering the Arctic Circle, is known as the **tundra**. The climate here is one of the harshest on earth, with long, cold winters and short summers. The soil in the tundra is permanently frozen.

South of the tundra is a huge forested area called the *taiga*, which extends across the whole of central Russia. The land here is frozen throughout winter. In summer, the top layer melts, forming pools and marshes. Below the *taiga* is a narrow band of flat grasslands, known as **steppes**. Winters here bring cold winds, snow and very long, dark nights. Summer brings hot, dry winds. In the autumn, cold rains turn the rich soil of the steppes into seas of mud.

Most of the land in Russia is flat.

Further south are mountains and semi-desert. The weather here is milder. A narrow strip of land along the Black Sea has a warm climate with long, sun-filled summers.

Some of the world's longest rivers are found in Russia. The wide Volga River flows through European Russia before emptying into the Caspian Sea. The Ob, Yenisei and Lena rivers flow north through Siberia to the Arctic Ocean.

The Central Caucasus mountain range in southern Russia.

Average temperatures

	January	July
St Petersburg	−9°C/16°F	17°C/63°F
Moscow	−9°C/16°F	19°C/66°F
Volgograd	−10°C/14°F	24°C/82°F
Astrakhan	−45°C/−49°F	17°C/63°F
Yakutsk	−60°C/−76°F	25°C/77°F

Lake Baikal, in Siberia, is the oldest and deepest lake in the world. It holds one-fifth of the earth's supply of fresh water. There are 2,000 different types of plants and animals living in the lake. Some people even believe it has its own lake monster! Once the waters of Lake Baikal were crystal clear. Now pollution is causing the fish and plants to die.

Plants and animals

The northern tundra is made up of flat, treeless plains. Nothing grows here but small shrubs, grasses, lichens and moss. The *taiga* is the world's largest forest. The most common trees are **conifers**, such as Siberian larches, pine, fir and spruce. Russia also has forests containing a mix of evergreen conifers and **deciduous** trees such as oak and birch.

Reindeer, wolves and brown bears still live in the northern forests. Deer, lynx, squirrels, moles and Siberian tigers are found in the mixed forests. Siberian tigers have even been known to wander into the suburbs of Vladivostock, in the far east. Leopards, cheetahs, porcupines, gazelles, wild goats and a type of antelope called chamois live in the semi-desert areas of the south.

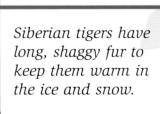

Siberian tigers have long, shaggy fur to keep them warm in the ice and snow.

*Many species of animals, like this European bison, are in danger of **extinction**. Pollution is killing their forest homes, and hunters try to trap them for their fur. There are now over 140 nature reserves in Russia, where animals can roam freely. Some of these have breeding programs to help increase the number of animals living in the wild.*

Animals living in Russian forests adapt to their food supply being frozen for many months of the year. Red squirrels collect pine cones and nuts in the summer and bury them in the earth. These high-energy snacks keep them alive through winter.

Wolves live in the northern forests.

Cities and landmarks

Moscow is Russia's largest city. Although it didn't become our capital city until 1918, Moscow is an old, old city. Eight hundred years ago, settlers on the north bank of the Moskva River built a *kreml,* or walled fortress. Inside its walls were churches, a palace and **arsenals** full of weapons. Today, the Moscow Kremlin is the home of our government. It contains magnificent churches and cathedrals, museums, government offices and a royal palace. Outside the Kremlin are many more churches and gracious buildings, including the colorful St. Basil's Cathedral. But there are also many ugly concrete apartment buildings.

The Kremlin, in the middle of Moscow, is an old fortress that now serves as the center of government.

St. Basil's Cathedral, in Red Square, was built in the 1500s. It has nine chapels, each with its own highly decorated roof.

Until 1917, Russian rulers spent their winters in the beautiful Winter Palace in St. Petersburg. It is now home to the Hermitage Museum, which contains the world's largest collection of art. Visitors come from all around the world to admire the paintings by European masters such as Rembrandt, Picasso and Matisse. It also has art from Siberia and central Asia, and works from ancient Greece and Rome.

St. Petersburg is Russia's second-largest city. It was planned and built by Peter the Great to be a meeting point for Russian and other European countries. St. Petersburg was called Leningrad under the communist government, after the leader Vladimir Lenin. Novgorod is our oldest city, 200 kilometers (124 miles) south of St. Petersburg. It was first settled around AD 800, and has many historic buildings, including its own kremlin.

Industry and agriculture

Before the Russian **Revolution** in 1917, Russia was a poor, undeveloped country. More people worked on farms than in factories. Under Soviet rule, the country became one of the most powerful nations in the world. Soviet citizens were told by the communist government that everything belonged to the state. Many new factories were built and existing ones were upgraded. Farms became bigger and more modern. Russia began to use its huge reserves of natural resources, such as timber, iron ore, oil, coal, diamonds and precious metals.

State-owned factories were set up in Moscow and St. Petersburg. They were also built in cities along the Volga River and in the Ural Mountains region. Instead of producing **consumer goods** that people needed in their homes, like televisions and washing machines, the factories produced iron, steel and heavy machinery. Money was invested in weapons and space research while people went without cars and telephones.

When the Soviet Union broke up in 1991, many of the government-controlled industries became privately owned. The people who ran the factories were given more say in what they could make. But there are still many shortages of consumer goods in Russia.

Timber production is a huge industry in Russia. Each year millions of acres of forest in Siberia's taiga are cut down to make paper and building materials.

Many people living in cities grow their own vegetables on small plots of land in the country. These are called dachas.

Land use in Russia

Farmed land	25%
Unfarmable land	30%
Forests	45%

Farming

Although Russia is a huge country, its climate is so cold and its soil so poor that only small areas can be used for farming. There is never enough food available to feed all the people. It is also difficult to transport the food from the farming areas to the cities. Sometimes fruit and vegetables are thrown away because they rot before they reach the markets and shops.

Under Soviet rule, all farms were owned by the state. Some farms had a mixture of crops and animals, while other, larger farms concentrated on one thing. In the 1980s, the government realized that farmers would produce more goods if they worked for themselves. Now there are many private farms in Russia.

Transportation

The best way to travel in Russia is by train. Our country is so big that there are huge distances between cities. Not many people can afford cars or gasoline. Even if they could, the road system is very poor. Our very cold climate means that in spring, when the winter snow starts to thaw, road surfaces begin to break up. Roads become boggy stretches of mud, impossible to drive on. That is why twice as much freight is sent by rail as by truck.

The Trans-Siberian Railway, which opened in 1914, is the longest railway line in the world. It stretches all the way from Moscow in the west to Vladivostock in the east, a distance of 9,300 kilometers (5,780 miles). People live close to the railway line because there are few roads in Siberia. The BAM line (Bailal-Amur-Mainline) was built in the 1980s so that workers could more easily get to the iron ore, uranium, gold, diamonds and other resources in this part of Siberia.

Trains on the Trans-Siberian Railway have different types of sleeping cabins. 'Soft class' has comfortable beds and armchairs, while 'hard class' has rows of bunk beds. The journey from one end of the line to the other takes a week.

Most people in Moscow get around on foot.

Rivers, such as the Volga, are also used to transport goods and raw materials around the country. The Volga is linked by a series of canals to the Black Sea, the River Don, the Baltic Sea, and the Moskva River in Moscow. The weather is so cold in many parts of Russia that the rivers and seaports freeze. **Ice-breakers** are used to keep things moving, but the most northerly ports are closed between November and March. Our main ports are St. Petersburg, Archangelsk, Nakhodka, Murmansk and Vladivostock.

Aeroflot is the national airline of Russia.

History and government

Russia was first settled around AD 500 by a group of people, called Slavs, who originally came from central Asia. Groups of Slavs were united around AD 900 by princes of a Slavic state called Rus. Kiev became the capital of Rus. In 1242, Kiev was attacked by Attars from central Asia. They burned the city to the ground and took control of Rus for more than 250 years, cutting its people off from the rest of Europe.

The Attars were defeated by a group of princes in 1380. Russia was then ruled by **czars**. Around 1550, Ivan the Terrible expanded the borders of the empire to the west and east. In the 1700s, under the rule of Peter the Great, Russia became an important European power. Architects and engineers were brought to Russia to modernize the cities. However, the people working on farms, known as **serfs**, received little help. They rose up against the czars, demanding better conditions.

In 1812, Russia was attacked by the French emperor Napoleon Bonaparte, but his troops were driven out. Russia expanded again, this time southwards. By the end of the 1800s, it was one of the largest empires in the world.

A statue of Lenin, who took power after the Russian Revolution in 1917, outside the Finland Station in St. Petersburg.

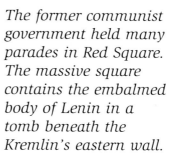

The former communist government held many parades in Red Square. The massive square contains the embalmed body of Lenin in a tomb beneath the Kremlin's eastern wall.

Revolution

The czars treated their people like slaves. During World War 1, Russia fell into chaos. Its armies began losing battles, and there was no food to feed the people. Workers began to riot. The Russian Revolution took place in 1917 when soldiers in Petrograd, now called St. Petersburg, forced the ruling czar to **abdicate**. A temporary government was set up. In 1922, Vladimir Lenin, a communist, set up the Union of Soviet Socialist Republics, the **USSR**. People were forced to hand over their land to the government. Anyone who spoke out against the new government was put in prison or killed.

After many years of struggle and poverty, Mikhail Gorbachev became the new leader. He introduced a new concept called *glasnost,* which means 'openness'. For the first time, people were able to have a say in how they wanted to live their lives.

In 1991, the Soviet Union was dissolved. Russia and the other 14 republics became separate nations, although they kept loose ties with each other by forming the Commonwealth of Independent States. This contains all the former Soviet republics except Estonia, Latvia and Lithuania. Although Russia still has many problems ahead, there is hope that things will improve in the future.

Fact file

Official name Russian Federation		**Population** 150,000,000	**Land area** 17,100,000 square kilometers (6.7 million square miles)
Government federation	**Languages** Russian (official); more than 140 other languages and dialects		**Religions** Christianity (Russian Orthodox, Roman Catholic, Protestant), Islam, Judaism, Buddhism
Currency Rouble (R)		**Capital city** Moscow	**Major cities** St. Petersburg, Nizhniy Novgorod, Novosibirsk, Ekaterinaburg, Samara, Omsk
		Climate varies from bitterly cold to hot and humid	
Major rivers Lena, Ob, Irtysh, Volga	**Deepest lake** Lake Baikal 1,753 meters (5,752 feet) deep		**Highest mountain** Mount Elbrus 5,642 meters (18,511 feet)
Main farm products grain, sugar beet, sunflower seeds, meat, dairy products	**Main industries** manufacturing (heavy machinery, cars, trucks, tractors, planes, electrical equipment), chemicals, oil refining, processed food, paper, textiles		**Natural resources** petroleum, iron ore, coal, diamonds, natural gas, timber, furs, precious metals

Glossary

abdicate	to step down from ruling a country
arsenals	places where weapons are stored
communism	a system of government where all property is owned by the state
conifers	trees with needle-like leaves
consumer goods	things made by industry that people want to buy
czar	a Russian emperor or king (the last czar ruled until 1917)
deciduous	plants and trees that lose their leaves in winter
exiled	forced to leave their country
extinction	when no more animals of this kind are left on earth
ice-breakers	ships that break up frozen rivers and seas
icons	religious paintings of Jesus Christ or of a saint
Lent	a special time of prayer and fasting leading up to Easter
playwright	a writer of plays
revolution	a rebellion that overthrows a ruler or government
Russian Empire	A large kingdom that covered what is now Russia, as well as areas to the west and south. It existed from the mid-1500s to 1917
serfs	peasants who worked on farms
steppes	a large area of flat land
taiga	the Russian word for the large belt of forests across the center of the country
tundra	the frozen, treeless wasteland area of the north
USSR	The large nation in eastern Europe and northern Asia that was made up of 15 republics. It existed from 1922 to 1991

Index